INTIMACY WITH THE Lord

The mystery of Union, Abiding, and One Spirit with God

PETER LENGWE

All Scripture quotations are taken from the New King James Version® (NKJV).

Printed in the United States of America

ISBN:
Softcover: 978-1-972299-63-0
Hardback: 978-1-972299-64-7
eBook: 978-1-972299-62-3

For permission requests, visit and write to the publisher at:

Peter Lengwe | THE BREAD OF LIFE GLOBAL MINISTRIES

ABOUT THE AUTHOR

Peter Lengwe is a Christian author and Bible teacher with a deep passion for the Word of God and the mystery of Christ revealed in Scripture. His writings flow from years of prayer, study, and personal pursuit of intimacy with the Lord, with a strong emphasis on biblical theology, spiritual union, and life in the Holy Spirit.

Known for presenting Scripture line upon line and theme upon theme, Peter's work calls believers beyond surface-level Christianity into a life of abiding, surrender, and transformation. His teaching consistently points readers back to God's original design—to live not from self, but from Christ who lives within.

Intimacy with the Lord reflects his central conviction: that Christianity is not merely believing in Christ, but participating in His life, until the Church becomes a dwelling place for God and the Bride is made ready for eternal union with the Bridegroom.

PREFACE

INTIMACY WITH THE LORD

There are mysteries in the Word of God that are not meant to be explained casually, approached lightly, or handled with theological distance. They are revealed only to those who are willing to draw near, to lay aside familiarity, and to allow the Spirit of God to speak beyond the limits of religious language. Intimacy with the Lord is such a mystery.

This book was not born out of curiosity, intellectual pursuit, or the desire to say something new. It was birthed from wrestling with Scripture, lingering in prayer, and encountering truths that refused to remain silent. As I journeyed through the Word, two passages began to burn in my spirit—1 Corinthians 6:17 and Matthew 19:5. At first glance, they appear to speak of two different realms: one spiritual, the other physical. Yet the deeper I went, the clearer it became that they are not separate revelations, but two sides of one eternal truth.

"But he who is joined to the Lord is one spirit with Him."
(1 Corinthians 6:17, NKJV)

"For this reason a man shall leave his father and mother and be joined to his wife, and the two shall become one flesh."
(Matthew 19:5, NKJV)

These verses are not merely illustrative—they are revelatory. One speaks of spiritual union, the other of physical union, yet both reveal the same divine intention: oneness through union. The apostle Paul later calls this truth "a great mystery"—one that ultimately points to Christ and the Church.

In this book, I have deliberately used the word intercourse. This choice is intentional and prayerful. It is not meant to shock, offend, or provoke carnality, but to restore depth to a word that Scripture itself reveals through pattern, shadow, and fulfillment. Intercourse, at its core, means exchange, union, participation, and shared life. It speaks of a mingling so complete that separation becomes impossible without death. Intimacy is the atmosphere; intercourse is the act of union.

From the beginning, God revealed His intentions through creation itself. Humanity was not created randomly, nor was male and female an afterthought. In Genesis, we are shown a profound truth: humanity was created as one, then revealed as two, so that union could be pursued, desired, and restored. The physical act of marital union is not merely biological—it is theological. It is a living parable, teaching humanity how oneness is formed through covenantal union.

In the same way, spiritual union with God is not achieved through effort, performance, or religious discipline alone. It is realized through continual spiritual intercourse—the believer's spirit abiding, yielding, and participating in the life of the Spirit of God. To be one Spirit with the Lord is not poetic language; it is a present reality for those who live in Christ.

This book will take you on a journey—

from creation to consummation,

from shadow to substance,

from physical revelation to spiritual fulfillment.

We will explore what it means to be:

- One Spirit
- One Mind
- One Body
- One Love
- One Baptism
- One with Christ

We will walk through the words of Jesus in John 15, the revelations of John in his epistles, the crucified life revealed by Paul, and the eternal prayer of Christ in John 17—all pointing to one undeniable truth: God desires union, not distance; participation, not observation.

This is not a book to be rushed. It is a book to be received. Some pages may challenge long-held assumptions. Others may expose areas where intimacy has been replaced by activity. Still others may awaken a hunger you did not know how to name. My prayer is that as you read, you will not merely gain understanding—but that you will be drawn into deeper fellowship, deeper surrender, and deeper union with the Lord.

The mystery is not hidden because it is complicated.

It is hidden because it is holy.

May the Spirit of truth lead you gently, clearly, and deeply into this revelation—until intimacy is no longer a concept you understand, but a union you live.

"The secret of the LORD is with those who fear Him, and He will show them His covenant."
—Psalm 25:14 (NKJV)

INTRODUCTION

The Eternal Call to Union

The story of Scripture is not merely the story of redemption from sin—it is the story of restoration to union. From Genesis to Revelation, the Word of God unveils a single, unbroken divine intention: God desires to dwell with humanity in oneness, not at a distance, not through intermediaries alone, but through shared life, shared Spirit, and shared glory.

This truth has often been approached cautiously, sometimes fragmented, and at times reduced to theological language that explains about God without leading the believer into God. Yet the Scriptures themselves speak boldly, plainly, and profoundly about union—a union so complete that it can only be described in terms of oneness.

"But he who is joined to the Lord is one spirit with Him."
(1 Corinthians 6:17, NKJV)

This statement by the apostle Paul is not metaphorical. It is not symbolic language meant merely to inspire devotion. It is a theological declaration of spiritual reality. To be joined to the Lord is to share in His life, His Spirit, His nature, and His purpose. Christianity, at its core, is not a belief system—it is participation in divine life.

To understand this, we must return to the foundation upon which God chose to reveal this mystery: creation itself.

When God created humanity, He did not begin with separation, but with oneness. Humanity was made in the image and likeness of God—a God who exists eternally in communion. Male and female were not created to establish hierarchy, competition, or independence, but to reveal unity through distinction. The language of Genesis does not merely describe biology; it unveils theology through embodiment.

"Therefore a man shall leave his father and mother and be joined to his wife, and they shall become one flesh."
(Genesis 2:24; Matthew 19:5, NKJV)

Jesus Himself returned to this foundational text to explain not only marriage, but permanence, covenant, and divine intent. The physical union of husband and wife was never meant to stand alone—it was designed as a living parable, a visible expression of an invisible truth. What is revealed in the flesh points to what God intended in the spirit.

This is why Scripture dares to speak of union with God using language drawn from marriage, abiding, indwelling, and becoming one. The physical act of marital union—what Scripture treats with holiness and covenantal seriousness—serves as a shadow of a greater reality: the joining of the human spirit to the Spirit of God.

The New Testament reveals that what was introduced in creation is fulfilled in Christ. Through His incarnation, death, resurrection, and the outpouring of the Holy Spirit, God did not merely forgive sin—He made union possible. The veil was torn not so humanity could visit God occasionally, but so God could dwell within humanity continually.

"Christ in you, the hope of glory."
(Colossians 1:27, NKJV)

This indwelling reality is the heart of the gospel. Salvation is not the end goal—it is the doorway. Justification restores right standing. Sanctification restores alignment. Union restores intimacy. The believer is not called merely to follow Christ externally, but to live from Christ internally.

In this book, the language of intimacy will often give way to the deeper language of union. Intimacy speaks of closeness; union speaks of shared life. Intimacy can be felt; union must be lived. This is why the Scriptures speak of abiding, walking in the Spirit, being led by the Spirit, being baptized into one body, and being transformed from glory to glory. All these expressions describe a life that flows from ongoing communion, not occasional encounter.

The words of Jesus in John 15 are central to this understanding:

"Abide in Me, and I in you."

Abiding is not passive rest—it is continual participation. It is the posture of one who no longer lives independently, but dependently; no longer self-sustained, but Spirit-sustained. To abide is to allow divine life to flow without obstruction. Apart from this union, Jesus declares, "you can do nothing."

The apostle John echoes this revelation in his epistles, linking union with God to walking in light, loving one another, overcoming the world, and manifesting divine life through obedience. Paul takes the revelation even further, declaring that the believer has been crucified with Christ, that Christ now lives in them, and that the Church is being formed into one Body—animated by one Spirit, moving with one purpose, and destined for one eternal union with the Lord.

This introduction sets the theological foundation for everything that follows. What you are about to explore is not speculative theology, nor mystical abstraction, but biblical revelation woven consistently through Scripture. Each chapter will build upon this foundation, drawing line upon line, precept upon precept, until the picture becomes clear: God's ultimate desire is oneness with His people.

This is not an invitation to knowledge alone.

It is an invitation to participation.

Not merely to understand union, but to enter it.

Not merely to speak of intimacy, but to live in continual communion with the Lord.

As you continue, approach these truths with reverence, humility, and hunger. The mystery you are about to explore is not distant—it is present. Not reserved for the future—it is available now.

"He who abides in love abides in God, and God in him."

May this journey draw you beyond form, beyond routine, and beyond religion—into the living reality of union with the Lord.

TABLE OF CONTENTS

CHAPTER ONE: The Eternal Origin of Union — Before the Foundation of the World

Before there was creation, before there was time, before there was dust from which man would be formed, there was union. The story of intimacy with the Lord does not begin in Genesis—it begins in eternity. To understand why humanity was created, why redemption was necessary, and why union with God is the ultimate aim of salvation, we must first return to what existed before the foundation of the world.

Scripture reveals that God did not create out of deficiency, loneliness, or need. God is eternally complete, eternally glorious, and eternally relational within Himself. Creation was not an attempt to fill a void; it was an overflow of divine life and love. The eternal God chose to share His life—to extend communion beyond Himself.

"According as He hath chosen us in Him before the foundation of the world..."
(Ephesians 1:4, NKJV)

This verse does not speak merely of foreknowledge—it speaks of preexistent intention. Humanity was chosen in Him, not merely for Him. Union was not an afterthought introduced after the fall; it was the original design.

Union Before Incarnation

Before Christ took on flesh, He existed in eternal fellowship with the Father. Jesus Himself prayed:

"And now, O Father, glorify Me together with Yourself, with the glory which I had with You before the world was."
(John 17:5, NKJV)

This glory was not merely radiance—it was shared life, shared presence, shared purpose. When Jesus later prays that believers would be one "just as We are one" (John 17:21), He is not introducing a new idea. He is inviting humanity into an ancient fellowship.

The call to union is therefore not human-centered; it is God-initiated. Redemption does not elevate humanity beyond its design—it restores humanity to its design.

Created as Spirit Before We Were Flesh

Scripture affirms that God is Spirit, and those who worship Him must do so in spirit and truth. Humanity, made in God's image, was therefore created with a spiritual capacity for communion. Though formed from the dust, man became a living being when God breathed into him the breath of life. That breath was not mere oxygen—it was participatory life.

This is why Scripture later declares:

"The spirit of man is the lamp of the LORD."
(Proverbs 20:27, NKJV)

The human spirit was designed as a vessel—capable of receiving, carrying, and responding to divine presence. Union with God was not meant to be external, distant, or occasional. It was meant to be internal, continual, and relational.

Why Creation Required Separation

If union was the eternal design, why then separation? Why creation, distinction, and distance?

Because union cannot be forced—it must be chosen.

God created humanity with the capacity to love, and love requires freedom. Freedom requires distinction. Distinction requires the possibility of separation. Thus, creation introduced space—not to eliminate union, but to make it meaningful.

The fall did not destroy God's desire for union; it distorted humanity's ability to sustain it. Sin did not merely break rules—it fractured communion. The greatest loss in the fall was not the garden—it was intimacy with God.

Redemption as Restoration to Union

The gospel is often preached as rescue from judgment, but Scripture reveals it as restoration to fellowship.

"God was in Christ reconciling the world to Himself."
(2 Corinthians 5:19, NKJV)

Reconciliation is relational language. It speaks of restored access, renewed trust, and shared presence. Through Christ, God did not merely forgive sin—He reopened the way for indwelling union.

This is why the tearing of the veil was so significant. It symbolized the end of distance. God was no longer confined to a place; He would now dwell within a people.

Union as the Goal of Salvation

Salvation is not the conclusion—it is the beginning of union.

- Justification restores legal standing
- Regeneration restores spiritual life
- Sanctification restores alignment
- Union restores shared existence

The believer is not called merely to imitate Christ, but to participate in His life.

"Christ in you, the hope of glory."
(Colossians 1:27, NKJV)

This indwelling reality fulfills the eternal purpose of God—to have a people who live from Him, through Him, and with Him.

The Church Foreknown as the Body

Scripture reveals that the Church was not a reaction to Israel's failure, nor a temporary solution in God's plan. The Church was foreknown, chosen, and destined to become one Body—animated by one Spirit and joined to one Head.

"For we are members of His body, of His flesh and of His bones... This is a great mystery, but I speak concerning Christ and the church."

(Ephesians 5:30–32, NKJV)

Here, Scripture unapologetically uses bodily and marital language to describe spiritual union. This is not poetic excess—it is theological precision. God uses the deepest human experience of union to reveal the depth of divine communion.

The Eternal Invitation

From eternity past, God's invitation has remained unchanged:

- Not visit Me, but abide in Me
- Not serve Me at a distance, but live from Me
- Not know about Me, but be joined to Me

This chapter establishes the foundation upon which everything else rests: union with God is not the reward of spiritual maturity—it is the reason for creation itself.

What unfolds in the chapters ahead is not a progression toward something new, but a return to something ancient—the eternal intention of God to dwell with His people in oneness.

"Behold, the dwelling place of God is with men."

The mystery begins in eternity.

The revelation unfolds in Christ.

The fulfillment continues in those who abide.

CHAPTER TWO: CREATION AS REVELATION — ONE MADE TWO TO BECOME ONE

Creation is not merely the beginning of history; it is the unveiling of divine intention. In Genesis, God does not only create the world—He reveals Himself, His nature, and His purpose through the way He creates. What God does in creation is intentional, ordered, and prophetic. Nothing is accidental. Nothing is arbitrary. Everything is instructional.

To understand intimacy with the Lord, we must see creation not as biology alone, but as theology embodied. Genesis is not simply telling us how things came into being—it is revealing why.

Humanity Created in the Image of a Relational God

"Then God said, 'Let Us make man in Our image, according to Our likeness.'"
(Genesis 1:26, NKJV)

The first revelation concerning humanity is not function, vocation, or authority—it is image. Humanity is created in the image of a God who speaks in plurality, fellowship, and communion. The God revealed in Scripture is not solitary; He is relational within Himself. Therefore, the image of God in humanity must necessarily include the capacity for relationship, union, and shared life.

"So God created man in His own image; in the image of God He created him; male and female He created them."
(Genesis 1:27, NKJV)

Notice the language: man is created, yet male and female are revealed. Scripture presents humanity first as one, then as two. This is not contradiction—it is revelation. Unity precedes distinction. Oneness exists before differentiation.

One Humanity, Revealed as Two

Genesis 2 takes us deeper, slowing the narrative to reveal meaning.

"And the LORD God formed man of the dust of the ground, and breathed into his nostrils the breath of life; and man became a living being."
(Genesis 2:7, NKJV)

Here we see the union of heaven and earth—dust and breath, body, and spirit. Humanity is not merely physical nor merely spiritual; humanity is both, designed to be the meeting place of divine and earthly realities. This alone prepares us to understand why humanity would later become the dwelling place of God by His Spirit.

Yet something profound follows.

"And the LORD God said, 'It is not good that man should be alone; I will make him a helper comparable to him.'"
(Genesis 2:18, NKJV)

This is not loneliness in the emotional sense—Adam is walking with God. This is incompleteness in expression. Humanity, as one, contains within it the revelation of two. What God does next is not corrective—it is revelatory.

The Separation That Teaches Union

God causes a deep sleep to fall upon the man. This is the first recorded sleep in Scripture, and it carries prophetic weight. In this sleep, God performs the first separation.

"And He took one of his ribs, and closed up the flesh in its place."
(Genesis 2:21, NKJV)

The woman is not created from the dust as the man was. She is taken out of the man. This reveals an essential truth: separation does not imply inferiority—it implies origin. The woman shares the same substance, life, and nature as the man.

When Adam awakens, his response is not analytical—it is revelatory:

"This is now bone of my bones and flesh of my flesh."
(Genesis 2:23, NKJV)

Adam recognizes her not as other, but as self revealed. This is critical. Union is not the joining of strangers; it is the reunion of what shares one origin.

Theological Meaning of "One Flesh"

Scripture then declares:

"Therefore a man shall leave his father and mother and be joined to his wife, and they shall become one flesh."
(Genesis 2:24, NKJV)

This statement is not merely descriptive—it is prescriptive. It reveals a divine principle. The word joined carries the meaning of being bound, cleaved, and united permanently. One flesh speaks not only of physical intimacy, but of shared life, shared identity, and shared existence.

This is why Scripture consistently treats sexual union as sacred. It is not casual because it is creationally powerful. In the joining of male and female, God reveals how oneness is formed through covenantal union.

Marriage is therefore not merely social—it is theological. It is God's chosen model to teach humanity about union through love, surrender, and participation.

Now this is how I perceive this union of husband and wife and it's profoundly essential to understanding the meaning of one flesh, the only time the husband and wife become one flesh is when they are in a state of intercourse; husband joining himself to the wife become one man as Adam was one man before the Lord took out eve from the man Adam creating in separation male and female.

The first man created had both male and female organism, the only thing the Lord God did was to mold a body and put the female organism in the molded body and thus God created them male and female. In the same manner scripture say in 1 corinthians 6:17; But the one who joins himself to the Lord is one spirit with Him.

When a believer joins himself or herself to the Lord in perpetual intercourse become one spirit with the Lord. And the same applies to the church of God which is body of Christ that will be joined to the Lord at His coming, the Lord becoming all in all in Himself. As the apostle Paul rightly calls it the greatest mystery.

Why God Chose the Physical to Reveal the Spiritual

Why would God use something as tangible and intimate as physical union to teach spiritual truth?

Because spiritual realities must be learned through embodiment.

The invisible God chose visible means to reveal invisible truths. Just as bread and wine reveal communion, so marriage reveals union. The physical act of becoming one flesh teaches humanity how separation is overcome through giving, receiving, and mutual yielding.

This is why the apostle Paul later draws directly from Genesis when speaking of Christ and the Church.

"For we are members of His body, of His flesh and of His bones... This is a great mystery, but I speak concerning Christ and the church." (Ephesians 5:30–32, NKJV)

Paul does not hesitate to apply marital language to spiritual union. He does so because marriage was designed from the beginning to point beyond itself.

Creation as Prophecy

Genesis is not only history—it is prophecy.

- One made two reveals distinction
- Two becoming one reveals union
- Union producing life reveals fruitfulness

This pattern unfolds throughout Scripture:

- Christ leaves heaven and cleaves to humanity

- The Spirit is given to indwell believers
- The Church becomes one Body
- The Bride is prepared for the Bridegroom

What begins in creation finds fulfillment in redemption and consummation in glory.

The Deeper Implication

Union requires:

- Separation from independence
- Leaving former identities
- Cleaving in covenant
- Yielding in love

This is true in marriage, and it is true in spiritual life. Just as husband and wife do not become one flesh by proximity, so believers do not become one Spirit with the Lord by association. Union requires participation.

Creation teaches us this truth gently but firmly:

Oneness is not automatic—it is entered through covenantal surrender.

Preparing for Spiritual Union

This chapter lays the groundwork for understanding why Scripture dares to speak of believers as:

- One Spirit with the Lord
- Members of His Body

- The Bride of Christ

What God revealed in the flesh was always meant to guide humanity toward what He desired in the spirit.

Creation was the lesson.

Christ is the fulfillment.

Union is the goal.

CHAPTER THREE: THE FALL — FRACTURED COMMUNION AND THE LOSS OF UNION

The fall of humanity was not merely a moral failure; it was a relational rupture. Sin did not begin with disobedience—it began with distance. What was fractured in Eden was not simply innocence, but union. The most devastating consequence of the fall was not death as an event, but separation as a condition—the breaking of communion between God and the human spirit.

To grasp the depth of redemption, we must first understand the depth of what was lost.

From Communion to Distance

Before the fall, humanity lived in unmediated fellowship with God. Scripture describes God walking in the garden "in the cool of the day"

(Genesis 3:8), language that speaks of habitual presence, not occasional visitation. There was no veil, no fear, no hiding. God's presence was not overwhelming—it was home.

Yet the moment sin entered, something immediate and tragic occurred:

"Then the eyes of both of them were opened, and they knew that they were naked."
(Genesis 3:7, NKJV)

This "opening of eyes" was not enlightenment—it was alienation. They became self-aware without God-awareness. Consciousness turned inward. Independence replaced dependence. Shame replaced openness.

Sin did not simply corrupt behavior; it reoriented the soul away from God.

The Birth of Separation

When God called out, "Where are you?" (Genesis 3:9), it was not because God lacked knowledge—it was because relationship had shifted. The question reveals the tragedy: humanity had moved from abiding presence to hiding posture.

"I was afraid... so I hid myself."

Fear entered where love once reigned. Self-preservation replaced surrender. The instinct to cover replaced the freedom to be seen.

This is the essence of the fall:

union replaced by distance, trust replaced by control, communion replaced by fear.

The Loss of Indwelling Life

Though humanity remained physically alive, something vital was lost. The human spirit—designed to be animated by the Spirit of God—became disconnected from its source. Life continued, but union ceased.

This is why Scripture later declares:

"In the day that you eat of it you shall surely die."

Death was not merely biological—it was spiritual separation. Humanity became alive to self but dead to God. The vessel remained, but the indwelling life was withdrawn.

Distortion of Desire

One of the most subtle effects of the fall was not the loss of desire, but the misdirection of desire. Humanity was still created for union but now sought it apart from God.

- Desire turned toward self-sufficiency
- Longing sought fulfillment through creation rather than Creator
- Intimacy was pursued without covenant
- Power was sought without submission

The serpent's temptation was not crude—it was theological:

"You will be like God..."

The lie was not about becoming divine but about becoming divine independently. Union was offered without surrender. Knowledge without communion. Power without presence.

This same distortion continues wherever spirituality seeks experience without obedience, intimacy without holiness, or union without lordship.

Marriage After the Fall

Even marriage, God's revealed model of union, was affected. What was meant to express mutual yielding now became marked by tension, domination, and self-interest. The union remained, but its purity was compromised.

This is why Scripture treats sexual sin with such seriousness—not because the act itself is evil, but because it misuses a holy capacity for union. What was designed to reveal covenant becomes destructive when severed from it.

Exile from the Garden

The removal from Eden was not punitive alone—it was protective.

"Lest he put out his hand and take also of the tree of life, and eat, and live forever..."

To live forever in a fallen state would be eternal separation. God's judgment was therefore also mercy. Humanity was expelled not from God's love, but from misaligned access to life.

The cherubim and flaming sword did not signify rejection—they signified guarded holiness. Access would one day be restored, but only through redemption, not rebellion.

The Ache That Remained

Though union was broken, the longing remained. Humanity carried within itself a memory of communion it could not fully articulate. This ache expresses itself in:

- Desire for intimacy
- Search for meaning

- Hunger for transcendence
- Restlessness of soul

As Ecclesiastes declares, God has set eternity in the human heart. The fall could not erase design—it could only distort expression.

Why Redemption Had to Be More Than Forgiveness

If the problem were merely guilt, forgiveness would suffice.

If the problem were merely behavior, instruction would suffice.

But the problem was separation.

Therefore, redemption had to restore:

- Access, not just pardon
- Indwelling, not just covering
- Union, not just innocence

This is why the promise of redemption always points beyond law to presence, beyond sacrifice to indwelling, beyond obedience to abiding.

The fall explains why humanity cannot return to God by effort. What was lost cannot be rebuilt from below—it must be restored from above.

A Promise Hidden in Judgment

Even in judgment, God spoke promise:

> *"The Seed of the woman shall bruise the serpent's head."*

Redemption would come not through human striving, but through divine intervention. God Himself would re-enter creation to restore what was lost—not merely to fix behavior, but to heal communion.

Preparing the Way for Union Restored

This chapter reveals why union must be given, not achieved; received, not earned. Humanity cannot climb back into Eden. God must come down into humanity.

The story now moves toward promise, covenant, and anticipation—a longing for restoration that echoes through the patriarchs, the law, the prophets, and the psalms.

Creation revealed union.

The fall fractured communion.

Redemption will restore oneness.

CHAPTER FOUR: PROMISE AND PATTERN — GOD'S RELENTLESS PURSUIT OF RESTORED COMMUNION

If the fall fractured communion, the rest of Scripture reveals God's relentless pursuit to restore it. From Eden onward, God does not retreat from humanity—He advances toward it. Though union was broken, God never abandoned His original intention. Instead, He began to reveal—progressively, patiently, and prophetically—the path back to oneness.

This chapter takes us deeper than promise alone. It uncovers pattern—because God does not restore union suddenly or randomly. He restores it orderly, through covenant, sacrifice, dwelling, and glory. Each stage is not the destination; each is a shadow preparing the soul for the fullness that would come in Christ.

God as the Initiator of Communion

From the moment humanity fell, God remained the pursuer.

- Adam hid — God called
- Humanity wandered — God covenanted
- Israel rebelled — God dwelt
- Sin separated — God descended

This reveals a foundational truth:

Communion with God is always initiated by God, never achieved by man.

"I will dwell among the children of Israel and will be their God."
(Exodus 29:45, NKJV)

The language of Scripture is unmistakably relational. God does not merely say, "I will rule" or "I will judge"—He says, "I will dwell."

Altars: The First Language of Restoration

The first visible response to the fall was sacrifice. Altars appear long before temples. Why? Because restored communion requires life for life.

- Abel's offering revealed approach through blood
- Noah's altar released divine pleasure
- Abraham's altars marked encounters, not rituals

Altars were not religious furniture; they were meeting places. Each altar testified to this truth:

Approach to God requires surrender of life, not self-improvement.

Yet altars could only restore momentary access, not permanent union.

Covenant: God Binding Himself to Humanity

With Abraham, God moves from altar to covenant.

"I will establish My covenant between Me and you... to be God to you."
(Genesis 17:7, NKJV)

Covenant is not contract—it is self-binding love. God does not merely promise blessings; He promises Himself.

Yet even covenant revealed limitation:

- God walked with Abraham
- God spoke to Moses
- God appeared among Israel

But He did not yet dwell within humanity.

The Tabernacle: God Dwelling Near but Not Within

The tabernacle marks a profound step forward in God's pursuit.

"Let them make Me a sanctuary, that I may dwell among them."
(Exodus 25:8, NKJV)

Notice the word: among, not within.

The tabernacle reveals something critical:

- God desires proximity
- But holiness requires separation
- Access is mediated
- Union is restricted

The veil stands as the great reminder:

God is present, but not accessible.

Only one man, once a year, with blood, could enter the Most Holy Place. This was not the fulfillment of union—it was a teaching tool.

The Priesthood: Intercourse Interrupted

The priest represented humanity before God—but representation is not union.

The high priest:

- Entered temporarily
- Exited quickly
- Never remained
- Never transformed fully

This reveals a painful truth:

Intercourse with God was interrupted, regulated, and external.

The system-maintained relationship, but it could not restore oneness.

The Glory: God Revealing His Desire to Dwell

Whenever God's glory descended—Sinai, the tabernacle, Solomon's temple—it overwhelmed human strength.

Why?

Because glory is the environment of union, and fallen humanity could not yet sustain it.

"The priests could not continue ministering because of the cloud."
(2 Chronicles 5:14, NKJV)

Glory exposed the gap:

- God desired to dwell
- Humanity could not host Him

This tension runs through the Old Testament like a groan.

The Prophets: God's Cry for Indwelling

The prophets begin to speak beyond external obedience toward internal transformation.

- "I will give you a new heart"
- "I will put My Spirit within you"
- "They shall all know Me"

These are not poetic hopes—they are prophetic necessities.

God was declaring:

Union will not come through law, sacrifice, or temple—but through indwelling.

Why the Law Could Never Produce Union

The law revealed holiness but could not impart life.

- It commanded righteousness
- But could not empower obedience
- It exposed sin
- But could not heal separation

The law kept humanity near God, but never in God.

"The law made nothing perfect."

Perfection requires union, not regulation.

The Hidden Promise: God Will Become the Dwelling Place

All these patterns whisper one truth:

God was not building a system—He was preparing a people.

- Altars taught surrender
- Covenant taught belonging
- Tabernacle taught holiness
- Priesthood taught mediation
- Glory taught desire

But Christ would bring union.

Why This Matters for Intimacy

Without understanding this chapter, intimacy becomes emotional, mystical, or subjective. But Scripture shows us something deeper:

- Intimacy without covenant is unsafe
- Access without holiness is impossible
- Experience without union is fleeting

God's pursuit has always been:

Not visitation, but habitation.

Not influence, but indwelling.

Not relationship at a distance, but oneness in Spirit.

The Stage Is Set

By the close of the Old Testament, humanity stands at the edge of revelation:

- A people prepared
- A hunger awakened

- A system exhausted
- A promise unresolved

The cry of the ages becomes clear:

Who will restore union?

Who will remove the veil?

Who will make God and man one again?

The answer does not come through another prophet, priest, or king.

It comes through God Himself entering flesh.

What Comes Next

Creation revealed union.

The fall fractured communion.

Promise and pattern prepared the way.

Now we move into the turning point of all history:

CHAPTER FIVE: THE INCARNATION — GOD ENTERING FLESH TO RESTORE UNION

All that came before—creation, fall, promise, pattern—was pointing toward a single, irreversible act in history: God entered flesh. The incarnation is not merely a miracle to be admired; it is the theological center of restoration. It is the moment when God did not simply speak to humanity, walk among humanity, or dwell near humanity—but became one with humanity.

The incarnation is God's definitive answer to fractured communion.

Why God Had to Become Flesh

Union could not be restored from humanity's side. The separation introduced by the fall was not external—it was internal. Humanity's nature had been compromised. The human spirit, once designed for indwelling communion, had become unable to host the fullness of God's presence.

Therefore, restoration required more than forgiveness. It required a new humanity.

"And the Word became flesh and dwelt among us."
(John 1:14, NKJV)

The phrase "dwelt among us" literally means "tabernacled". What the tabernacle symbolized externally, Christ embodied fully. God did not repair the old dwelling—He became the dwelling.

Christ as the Meeting Place

In Jesus Christ, heaven and earth were no longer separated by veils, sacrifices, or priesthoods. They were united in one Person.

- Fully God — uncreated, eternal, holy
- Fully man — created, temporal, embodied

This was not mixture or confusion; it was union without loss of identity. The divine nature did not absorb humanity, nor did humanity diminish divinity. Instead, perfect fellowship was restored within Christ Himself.

This is critical:

Union was restored in Christ before it was ever restored in us.

He is not merely the mediator of union—He is the model and source of it.

The Second Adam and a New Humanity

Scripture calls Jesus the last Adam. This is not symbolic language—it is ontological.

The first Adam was created for union and lost it.

The last Adam embodied union and secured it.

In Christ:

- Humanity is re-created
- Obedience is restored
- Communion is sustained
- Life flows without interruption

Jesus did not live for God at a distance; He lived from God in unbroken fellowship.

"I can do nothing of Myself... I always do those things that please Him."

This is not moral striving—it is union in operation.

Why Jesus Had to Live, Not Just Die

If the cross were the only necessity, Christ could have appeared, died, and returned to glory. But Scripture reveals something deeper: He had to live a human life in perfect union with God.

Why?

Because union had to be demonstrated, not merely declared.

- He lived by the Spirit
- He obeyed from intimacy
- He spoke what He heard
- He did what He saw

Jesus reveals what humanity looks like when union is restored.

The Cross: Union Carried Through Death

The cross is often preached as substitution—and it is—but it is also participation.

At the cross:

- Sin is judged
- The old humanity is crucified
- Separation is absorbed
- Death is entered

But more than that, union is preserved through death.

Jesus does not lose communion with the Father through obedience—even unto death. The cross proves that union with God is stronger than sin, suffering, or death itself.

"Father, into Your hands I commit My spirit."

Even in death, communion remains.

The Veil Torn: The End of Distance

When Christ breathed His last, something profound happened:

"Then the veil of the temple was torn in two from top to bottom."

This was not symbolic theater—it was spiritual declaration.

- The separation was removed
- Access was restored

- God was no longer confined
- Humanity was invited in

The tearing from top to bottom reveals divine initiative. God Himself opened the way. What centuries of sacrifice could not achieve, one obedient life accomplished.

Resurrection: Union Vindicated

The resurrection is not merely victory over death—it is the vindication of union.

Death could not hold Christ because union with God is life itself.

"In Him was life."

Resurrection declares:

- Union is indestructible
- Life flows eternally
- Humanity in Christ is now incorruptible

Jesus rises not as spirit alone, but as glorified humanity—the prototype of what redeemed humanity will become.

Ascension: Union Seated in Glory

The ascension reveals the final shock of the incarnation:

Humanity is now seated in heavenly places.

Not symbolically. Not metaphorically. Actually.

This means:

- Union is complete
- Humanity is represented eternally
- The door to participation is open

Christ does not shed His humanity when He ascends—He brings it with Him.

Why This Changes Everything

Because of the incarnation:

- Union is no longer theoretical
- Communion is no longer external
- Intimacy is no longer reserved

The believer is not called to admire Christ from afar, but to enter into what Christ has already accomplished.

Salvation is not Christ living for us alone—it is Christ living in us.

The Transition to Indwelling

The incarnation restores union objectively.

The next step restores union subjectively.

Christ entered flesh so the Spirit could later enter believers.

What was external in Christ would soon become internal in the Church.

Where We Go Next

Creation revealed union.

The fall fractured communion.

Promise prepared the way.

The incarnation restored union in Christ.

Now comes the most personal revelation of all:

CHAPTER SIX: THE INDWELLING SPIRIT — UNION MADE PERSONAL

What the incarnation restored objectively in Christ, the Holy Spirit now applies subjectively in the believer. The work of Christ did not end with ascension; it continued with indwelling. Union was not merely achieved for humanity—it was designed to be experienced within humanity. This is where intimacy ceases to be doctrine and becomes life.

The giving of the Spirit is not an add-on to salvation. It is the completion of God's eternal purpose.

From God With Us to God In Us

Jesus' earthly life revealed what union looks like in one Man. The outpouring of the Holy Spirit reveals God's intent to reproduce that union in many sons.

"It is to your advantage that I go away; for if I do not go away, the Helper will not come to you."

The advantage was not power alone—it was proximity. Christ beside them was good. Christ within them would be transformational.

The Spirit does not merely assist the believer; He inhabits the believer. This marks the greatest shift in redemptive history: God moves from dwelling near His people to dwelling inside His people.

The Spirit as the Agent of Union

The Holy Spirit is not a force, an influence, or an abstract presence. He is God Himself, given to make union possible, continual, and living.

- The Father planned union
- The Son secured union
- The Spirit administers union

Without the Spirit, union remains theoretical. With the Spirit, union becomes experiential and ongoing.

This is why Scripture declares that believers are one Spirit with the Lord. This is not imitation. It is participation.

Why Indwelling Was Necessary

If forgiveness were the only goal, the Spirit would not need to dwell within. But God's goal was not merely to remove guilt—it was to restore communion.

Indwelling accomplishes what law, sacrifice, and external obedience never could:

- Internal alignment of desire
- Continuous fellowship
- Shared life
- Sustained holiness

Holiness is not maintained by distance—it is sustained by presence.

The Human Spirit as God's Dwelling Place

From the beginning, humanity was designed as a habitation, not merely a servant. The breath of God in creation pointed to indwelling intention. The Spirit now fulfills that design.

"Do you not know that your body is the temple of the Holy Spirit...?"

The temple imagery is deliberate. God no longer dwells in structures made with hands. He dwells in living vessels. The believer becomes sacred space—not by effort, but by occupation.

This redefines identity:

- You are not merely forgiven
- You are not merely accepted
- You are inhabited

Intercourse as Continual Indwelling Fellowship

This is where the language of intercourse becomes essential.

Intercourse is not a moment—it is ongoing exchange. In the spiritual sense, it speaks of:

- Receiving divine life
- Yielding human will
- Sharing affection
- Participating in movement

The Spirit does not visit periodically; He abides continually. Spiritual intercourse is therefore not an event—it is a way of being.

When believers grieve the Spirit, it is not because rules were broken, but because fellowship was disrupted. Union remains, but communion is hindered.

Why the Spirit Must Lead, Not Assist

The Spirit was not given to improve human independence, but to replace it.

"For as many as are led by the Spirit of God, these are sons of God."

Sons do not live by instruction alone—they live by shared life. The Spirit does not shout commands from outside; He moves from within. This is the difference between servants and sons.

To resist the Spirit's leading is not merely disobedience—it is a refusal of union's expression.

The Spirit and the Crucified Life

Union with God requires the death of independence.

"I have been crucified with Christ; it is no longer I who live, but Christ lives in me."

The Spirit does not coexist with self-rule. Where Christ lives, self must yield. This is not loss—it is exchange.

- Self-life produces striving
- Spirit-life produces fruit
- Self-effort exhausts
- Spirit-intercourse sustains

The Spirit makes the crucified life livable by supplying divine life where human strength ends.

Abiding: The Language of Indwelling

Jesus describes union through one word: abide.

Abiding is not passive rest; it is active dependence. It is the continual posture of one who draws life from another. Branches do not strive to bear fruit—they remain connected.

The Spirit maintains that connection from the inside.

Without abiding, activity becomes religious. With abiding, obedience becomes organic.

The Spirit as the Seal of Future Union

The indwelling Spirit is also a guarantee. He is the down payment of what is coming.

What is now spiritual union will one day become visible consummation. The Church, already joined in Spirit, will be joined in glory. The Bride who knows the Bridegroom inwardly will meet Him outwardly.

The Spirit is preparing the Church not merely for service, but for marriage.

Why This Chapter Changes Everything

Without this revelation:

- Christianity becomes performance
- Holiness becomes pressure
- Intimacy becomes emotion
- Doctrine becomes distance

With this revelation:

- Life flows from union
- Obedience flows from love
- Holiness flows from presence
- Intimacy becomes continuous fellowship

The Spirit was given so that union would not end with Christ but multiply through the Body.

The Journey Forward

Creation revealed union.

The fall fractured communion.

Promise prepared the way.

The incarnation restored union in Christ.

The Spirit makes union personal and perpetual.

Now we must ask the next essential question:

How does this union express itself corporately?

CHAPTER SEVEN: One Body — Union Expressed Through the Church

Union with God was never intended to terminate at the individual. What begins personally through the indwelling Spirit must mature corporately through the Body. The mystery of intimacy with the Lord reaches one of its deepest expressions here: many becoming one without losing distinction. This is not organizational unity, denominational agreement, or shared doctrine alone—it is organic oneness born of shared life.

The Church is not an institution Christ founded; it is a Body Christ inhabits.

From One Spirit to One Body

Scripture never separates union with Christ from union with His people. To be joined to the Lord is to be joined to all who are joined to Him.

"For by one Spirit we were all baptized into one body—whether Jews or Greeks, whether slaves or free—and have all been made to drink into one Spirit."

This baptism is not water—it is incorporation. The Spirit does not merely dwell in believers individually; He weaves believers together corporately. One Spirit produces one Body because life shared must express itself collectively.

Union with Christ that refuses union with the Body is incomplete and immature.

The Church as an Organism, Not an Organization

The Church is described using living language:

- Body
- Bride
- Temple
- House
- Flock
- Family

These are not metaphors chosen for poetry—they are ontological descriptions. The Church lives because Christ lives in her. She moves because Christ animates her. She grows because Christ supplies her.

Organizations can function without life.

Bodies cannot.

This is why the Church cannot be sustained by programs, strategies, or charisma. She must be sustained by ongoing union with the Head.

Christ the Head — Source of All Life

Union in the Body is not horizontal first; it is vertical.

"He is the head of the body, the church... that in all things He may have the preeminence."

The Head is not symbolic leadership—it is life-source. Every function, gift, movement, and expression of the Body flows from connection to Christ.

Disconnection from the Head results in:

- Striving instead of flowing
- Imitation instead of expression
- Activity instead of fruit

True unity does not come from agreement among members, but from shared dependence on the Head.

Members, Not Individuals

Scripture never calls believers "independent units." It calls them members—parts of a whole.

A member:

- Does not exist for itself
- Has no life apart from the body
- Functions for the good of the whole

This is why spiritual independence is a contradiction. To say "Christ yes, the Body no" is to misunderstand union entirely. You cannot be one with the Head and severed from the Body.

Union produces interdependence, not isolation.

Spiritual Intercourse in the Corporate Sense

Here the language of intercourse deepens further.

Just as spiritual intercourse occurs between the believer and the Lord through continual exchange, corporate intercourse occurs within the Body through shared life, love, and submission.

This includes:

- Bearing one another's burdens
- Supplying what others lack
- Yielding personal preference
- Sharing spiritual life

Where the Body functions rightly, life flows freely. Where self dominates, flow is restricted.

Division is not merely disagreement—it is intercourse interrupted.

Why Love Is the Measure of True Unity

Scripture repeatedly anchors unity in love, not structure.

"By this all will know that you are My disciples, if you have love for one another."

Love is not sentiment—it is the circulation of divine life. Where love flows, unity follows. Where love is absent, unity becomes enforced or artificial.

Love is the evidence that the Body is alive and that Christ is present.

This is why unforgiveness, jealousy, pride, and rivalry are so destructive—they block the flow of life within the Body. They do not merely harm relationships; they hinder communion.

The Church as the Dwelling Place of God

Individually, believers are temples. Corporately, the Church becomes a habitation of God in the Spirit.

"You are being built together for a dwelling place of God."

Notice the language: together. God does not merely dwell in isolated stones—He dwells in a fitted structure. Living stones must be aligned, joined, and positioned.

A stone out of place cannot express the glory of the house.

One Body, Many Expressions

Unity does not erase diversity; it redeems it.

- Different gifts
- Different functions
- Different callings

Yet all serve one life.

Uniformity is not unity. True unity allows distinction while maintaining oneness of source and purpose. The eye does not become the hand, and the hand does not resent the foot. Each rejoices in its place because each is drawing from the same life.

The Bride Dimension of the Body

The Body is not only functional—it is relational.

Scripture reveals the Church not only as a Body but as a Bride. This brings us back to the language of union and intercourse. The Church is not merely working for Christ—she is being prepared for Him.

The Bride learns intimacy now so she may stand in union later.

- Submission is learned now
- Faithfulness is cultivated now
- Love is deepened now

Corporate union prepares the Church for eternal union.

Why the Enemy Attacks the Church

Satan does not fear individual believers as much as he fears a united Body. A lone branch can be cut. A living vine cannot.

Division is his greatest strategy because unity is God's greatest expression.

Where the Church walks in union:

- Authority is released
- Glory is manifested
- Christ is revealed

Hell, trembles where the Body functions as one.

The Goal of Corporate Union

The ultimate purpose of the Church is not influence, relevance, or expansion—it is expression of Christ.

"Till we all come to the unity of the faith... to a perfect man, to the measure of the stature of the fullness of Christ."

This is maturity: Christ fully formed in a people.

Not Christ admired.

Not Christ studied.

But Christ expressed.

Why This Chapter Is Pivotal

Without this revelation:

- Intimacy becomes private
- Spirituality becomes isolated
- Church becomes optional

With this revelation:

- Intimacy becomes shared
- Life becomes corporate
- Union becomes visible

The Church is the public manifestation of private union.

Where We Go Next

Union with God is personal.

Union with Christ is corporate.

Union with the Body is essential.

Now we must confront the great threat to union—the self-life.

CHAPTER EIGHT: ONE MIND — THE DEATH OF INDEPENDENCE AND THE RENEWAL OF UNION

Union with God can be received in the spirit, yet resisted in the mind. This is why many believers are indwelt by the Spirit, joined to the Lord, and part of the Body—yet still live fragmented lives. The battleground of union is not first the body, nor even the will; it is the mind. Until the mind is renewed, intimacy remains limited, and intercourse with God is continually interrupted.

God's desire is not merely that we think about Him correctly, but that we think with Him, from Him, and in alignment with Him.

Why the Mind Matters in Union

Scripture never treats the mind as neutral. The mind is either:

- A gateway for divine life

- Or a stronghold for self-rule

The fall did not only corrupt human behavior—it produced an independent consciousness. Humanity began to reason apart from God, interpret reality without God, and define good and evil autonomously. This is why Scripture consistently contrasts the mind of the flesh with the mind of the Spirit.

Union with God cannot be sustained where independence is preserved.

The Mind of the Flesh vs. the Mind of the Spirit

"For to be carnally minded is death, but to be spiritually minded is life and peace."

This is not a moral contrast alone; it is an ontological contrast.

- The fleshly mind operates from self-reference
- The spiritual mind operates from divine dependence

The fleshly mind asks, "What do I think?"

The spiritual mind asks, "What is the mind of the Lord?"

Death, in this sense, is not cessation of existence—it is disconnection from divine life. A believer can be spiritually alive and yet function mentally from death when the mind is governed by independence.

The Fall as a Shift in Consciousness

When Adam and Eve ate from the tree of the knowledge of good and evil, something profound happened:

they became self-interpreting beings.

Knowledge was no longer received relationally from God; it was possessed autonomously. The human mind became the final authority. This is the root of pride, rebellion, and spiritual resistance.

Redemption must therefore restore not only righteousness, but right dependence.

The Call to the Renewed Mind

"Do not be conformed to this world, but be transformed by the renewing of your mind."

Transformation does not begin with behavior modification—it begins with mental realignment. Scripture does not merely inform the renewed mind; it is submitted to the Spirit.

Renewal means:

- Unlearning independence
- Releasing control
- Yielding interpretation
- Receiving perspective

The renewed mind no longer insists on understanding before obeying. It trusts union over explanation.

The Mind of Christ

Scripture makes a radical declaration:

"But we have the mind of Christ."

This does not mean we merely imitate Christ's thinking—it means we participate in His consciousness through union. Christ lived in constant awareness of the Father. He did nothing independently, spoke nothing autonomously, and judged nothing from self.

This is the mind God intends for His people:

- A mind that listens

- A mind that discerns
- A mind that yields
- A mind that abides

The mind of Christ is the mental expression of spiritual union.

Why Independence Is the Enemy of Intimacy

Independence feels like strength, but it is the residue of the fall. God never designed humanity to be self-governing apart from Him. Independence resists:

- Submission
- Trust
- Waiting
- Obedience

True intimacy requires vulnerability, and vulnerability requires surrender. The independent mind cannot abide because it must control outcomes.

Union demands the death of the illusion of self-sufficiency.

The Crucified Mind

"I have been crucified with Christ; it is no longer I who live..."

This crucifixion is not only positional—it is practical. The self that must die is not merely sinful behavior, but self-rule. The renewed mind accepts crucifixion as liberation, not loss.

The crucified mind:

- No longer demands its own way

- No longer insists on its own understanding
- No longer interprets life without God

It lives by revelation, not reaction.

One Mind in the Body

Union in the Body requires shared perspective.

"Let this mind be in you which was also in Christ Jesus."

Disunity in the Church often begins not in doctrine, but in competing minds—preferences, ambitions, offenses, and self-interest. One Body cannot function with fragmented consciousness.

One Spirit seeks to produce one mind, not uniform thought, but unified submission.

The Renewed Mind as the Gateway to Peace

Peace is not the absence of conflict; it is the presence of alignment.

"And the peace of God... will guard your hearts and minds through Christ Jesus."

When the mind abides in union, peace becomes the governing atmosphere. Anxiety reveals divided trust. Fear reveals fractured dependence. Rest reveals intimacy preserved.

Spiritual Intercourse and the Mind

Spiritual intercourse with the Lord is sustained or interrupted by the mind.

- A surrendered mind keeps the channel open
- A resisting mind restricts flow
- A renewed mind cooperates with life

This is why Scripture calls believers to:

- Meditate
- Set the mind
- Fix the thoughts
- Take thoughts captive

Not to control God—but to remove resistance.

The Outcome of One Mind

Where the mind is renewed:

- Obedience becomes natural
- Discernment becomes clear
- Union becomes stable
- Fruit becomes inevitable

The believer no longer oscillates between intimacy and distance. Communion becomes consistent because resistance has been dismantled.

Why This Chapter Is Essential

Without a renewed mind:

- Union remains positional but not experiential
- Intimacy becomes emotional rather than spiritual
- The Church remains divided internally

With a renewed mind:

- Life flows freely
- Love governs responses

- Unity becomes sustainable

One Spirit seeks one Body.

One Body requires one mind.

One mind preserves union.

Where We Go Next

The renewed mind prepares the way for the next essential dimension of union:

CHAPTER NINE: ONE LOVE — THE CIRCULATION OF DIVINE LIFE

Union with God is sustained, expressed, and perfected by love. Love is not merely an attribute of God—it is the very life of God in motion. Where love flows, union is preserved. Where love is hindered, communion is interrupted. This is why Scripture consistently presents love not as an optional virtue, but as the essential environment of intimacy with the Lord.

Union can exist positionally through salvation yet fail experientially where love is resisted. Love is the circulation system of divine life. It is how God's life moves within the believer and through the Body.

"God is love, and he who abides in love abides in God, and God in him." (NKJV)

This is not poetic sentiment—it is theological precision. Abiding in God and abiding in love are inseparable realities.

Love as the Nature of Union

Union with God does not begin with love as an emotion; it begins with love as nature.

"We love Him because He first loved us." (NKJV)

Love originates in God, not in human response. The believer does not generate love toward God; the believer receives God's love, and that love then returns to God and flows outward to others.

This is why Scripture never commands believers to create love—but to abide in it.

Why Love Is the Greatest Commandment

Jesus summarizes the entire law with love—not because love replaces obedience, but because love fulfills obedience.

"You shall love the LORD your God with all your heart, with all your soul, and with all your mind." (NKJV)

"You shall love your neighbor as yourself." (NKJV)

These are not two separate loves. They are one love expressed in two directions. Love for God that does not flow toward others is incomplete. Love for others that does not flow from God is unsustainable.

Love is the evidence that union is alive.

The Cross — Love Proven, Union Secured

The cross is the highest revelation of love because it is the deepest expression of self-giving union.

"But God demonstrates His own love toward us, in that while we were still sinners, Christ died for us." (NKJV)

At the cross:

- Love absorbs judgment
- Love bears separation
- Love restores access

The cross reveals that union with God is not preserved by comfort, but by sacrificial love. This is why Jesus links love directly to obedience:

"If you love Me, keep My commandments." (NKJV)

Obedience does not produce love—love produces obedience.

Love as the Evidence of Indwelling

Scripture consistently presents love as the proof of God's indwelling presence.

"No one has seen God at any time. If we love one another, God abides in us, and His love has been perfected in us." (NKJV)

God's invisibility becomes visible through love. Where love is perfected, God is manifested. Where love is absent, intimacy is theoretical.

Love is not perfected through intensity—it is perfected through participation.

Why Love Preserves the Body

The Body of Christ does not fracture primarily through doctrinal error—it fractures through relational breakdown. This is why Scripture places such emphasis on love within the Body.

"By this all will know that you are My disciples, if you have love for one another." (NKJV)

Love is the distinguishing mark of true union. Gifts may impress, knowledge may inform, structure may organize—but love reveals Christ.

Where love flows freely:

- Offense loses power
- Pride is dismantled
- Unity is sustained

Love and the Flow of Spiritual Life

Love is the medium through which divine life circulates. Just as blood carries life through the body, love carries the life of God through the Church.

"And above all these things put on love, which is the bond of perfection." (NKJV)

The phrase bond of perfection reveals that love is what holds union together. Without love, union becomes positional but not functional.

This is why Scripture warns:

"Though I have all faith, so that I could remove mountains, but have not love, I am nothing." (NKJV)

Power without love does not build union—it bypasses it.

Love as the Safeguard of Intimacy

Love protects intimacy from corruption. Fear, control, manipulation, and self-interest cannot coexist with love.

"There is no fear in love; but perfect love casts out fear." (NKJV)

Fear signals distance. Love restores closeness. Where fear governs, union retreats. Where love governs, intimacy flourishes.

Love invites vulnerability—and vulnerability sustains communion.

One Love in One Body

The Church is called not merely to believe the same truths, but to love with the same love.

"Now may the God of patience and comfort grant you to be like-minded toward one another, according to Christ Jesus." (NKJV)

Unity of mind is sustained by unity of love. Agreement without love is fragile. Love without truth is unstable. Love rooted in truth produces lasting union.

Love as the Pathway to Maturity

Scripture presents maturity not as accumulation of knowledge, but as growth in love.

"Speaking the truth in love, may grow up in all things into Him who is the head—Christ." (NKJV)

Growth into Christ is growth into love. As love deepens, union strengthens. As union strengthens, fruit multiplies.

Why Love Is the Fulfillment of Union

Union without love would be mechanical. Love makes union relational, joyful, and life-giving.

"Now abide faith, hope, love, these three; but the greatest of these is love." (NKJV)

Love is greatest because it is eternal. Faith will become sight. Hope will be fulfilled. Love will remain because love is the life of God shared forever.

The Outcome of One Love

Where love governs:

- Intimacy is protected
- Unity is preserved

- The Spirit flows freely
- Christ is revealed

Love is not the reward of union—it is the expression of union.

Why This Chapter Matters

Without love:

- Union becomes theoretical
- Knowledge becomes pride
- Power becomes dangerous
- The Body becomes divided

With love:

- Union becomes experiential
- Obedience becomes joyful
- The Church becomes radiant

One Spirit produces one Body.

One Body lives by one Mind.

One Mind is sustained by one Love.

Where We Go Next

Love prepares the believer for abiding.

CHAPTER TEN: ABIDE IN ME — THE MYSTERY OF CONTINUAL COMMUNION

(John 15:5–6)

Union with God finds its daily expression in one word Jesus chose deliberately: abide. This is not poetic language, nor is it mystical abstraction. Abiding is the practice of union, the lived reality of intimacy, the continual flow of divine life between Christ and the believer. If union is the truth secured by Christ, abiding is how that truth is lived moment by moment.

Jesus does not invite His disciples into sporadic encounters, seasonal devotion, or emotional peaks. He calls them into unceasing communion.

"Abide in Me, and I in you." (NKJV)

This is the language of mutual indwelling—not visitation, not proximity, but shared life.

Abiding Is Mutual, Not One-Sided

Jesus does not say, “Abide near Me,” nor “Think about Me,” but “Abide in Me, and I in you.” This reveals a profound truth: abiding is reciprocal.

“Abide in Me, and I in you.” (NKJV)

Union is not maintained by human effort alone, nor by divine sovereignty alone—it is relational participation. Christ supplies life: the believer supplies yielded presence. Abiding is the posture of dependence that allows divine life to flow without obstruction.

The Vine and the Branch — Union Explained Simply

Jesus gives one of the clearest images of union in all of Scripture:

“I am the vine, you are the branches.” (NKJV)

This metaphor removes all illusion of independence. Branches do not generate life. They do not decide fruitfulness. They do not labor to produce sap. Their one responsibility is to remain connected.

“He who abides in Me, and I in him, bears much fruit.” (NKJV)

Fruit is not produced by striving—it is the natural consequence of union.

“Without Me You Can Do Nothing”

Jesus makes a statement that dismantles human self-confidence:

“For without Me you can do nothing.” (NKJV)

This is not exaggeration. It is theological reality. Nothing here does not mean inactivity; it means nothing of eternal value. Activity apart from union may impress people, but it cannot produce life.

The tragedy of much religious life is not sin—it is independence. The flesh can preach, organize, sing, build, and influence—yet still remain disconnected from divine life.

Abiding exposes the difference between:

- Work and fruit
- Effort and life
- Religion and union

Abiding as Spiritual Intercourse

Abiding is not passive waiting; it is continual exchange. This is where the language of spiritual intercourse finds its clearest expression.

In abiding:

- Christ gives life
- The believer yields will
- The Spirit facilitates communion
- Love sustains flow

Just as physical intercourse involves giving and receiving, so spiritual abiding involves constant participation. The believer draws life, truth, strength, and direction from Christ—not occasionally, but continuously.

Abiding is not something you visit—it is something you live in.

Why Fruitlessness Reveals Disconnection

Jesus speaks soberly about branches that do not abide:

"If anyone does not abide in Me, he is cast out as a branch and is withered." (NKJV)

Withering is not sudden—it is gradual. It begins when connection is neglected. The branch may still look attached outwardly, but inwardly the flow has stopped.

Fruitlessness is not always the result of rebellion; often it is the result of neglecting communion.

The Role of Pruning in Abiding

Abiding does not eliminate discipline—it invites purification.

"Every branch that bears fruit He prunes, that it may bear more fruit." (NKJV)

Pruning is not punishment—it is love protecting union. God removes what competes with life-flow. Anything that hinders intimacy—pride, distraction, self-sufficiency—must be cut away.

Pruning hurts only where attachment exists. It is proof that the branch belongs to the vine.

Abiding Through the Word

Jesus ties abiding directly to His Word:

"If you abide in Me, and My words abide in you, you will ask what you desire, and it shall be done for you." (NKJV)

The Word is not information—it is seed. When the Word abides, it shapes desire, aligns will, and purifies prayer. Asking becomes an extension of union, not an attempt to persuade God.

Answered prayer flows from shared intention, not religious formula.

Abiding and Obedience

Abiding is sustained by obedience—not legal obedience, but relational obedience.

"If you keep My commandments, you will abide in My love." (NKJV)

Obedience does not create love; it protects intimacy. Just as trust preserves marriage, obedience preserves communion. Disobedience does not end union, but it disrupts fellowship.

Love motivates obedience, and obedience safeguards love.

Abiding Produces Glory

Jesus reveals the ultimate purpose of abiding:

"By this My Father is glorified, that you bear much fruit." (NKJV)

God is glorified not when believers strive, but when divine life flows unhindered. Fruit reveals source. When fruit appears, the vine is honored.

The glory of God rests where union is visible.

Abiding as the Normal Christian Life

Abiding is not advanced spirituality—it is basic Christianity. Jesus does not present abiding as an option for the mature; He presents it as the only way to live.

Without abiding:

- Prayer becomes effort
- Obedience becomes heavy
- Love becomes strained
- Ministry becomes exhausting

With abiding:

- Prayer becomes natural
- Obedience becomes joyful

- Love becomes effortless
- Life becomes fruitful

Why This Chapter Is Central

This chapter stands at the heart of Intimacy with the Lord because it moves the reader from theology to practice, from truth to experience, from union declared to communion lived.

Union explains who you are.

Abiding determines how you live.

The Way Forward

Abiding teaches us how union is maintained daily, hourly, moment by moment.

Now we must go deeper still—into what sustains abiding when emotions fade and circumstances test communion.

CHAPTER ELEVEN: ABIDE IN MY WORD — DESIRE, PRAYER, AND UNION

(John 15:7)

If abiding is the posture of continual communion, then the Word is the channel through which that communion is stabilized, deepened, and safeguarded. Union with Christ is sustained not by emotion, experience, or circumstance, but by the indwelling Word. This is why Jesus does not separate abiding in Him from His Word abiding in us—they are one reality expressed in two directions.

"If you abide in Me, and My words abide in you, you will ask what you desire, and it shall be done for you." (NKJV)

This statement is one of the most misunderstood promises in Scripture—not because it is unclear, but because it is conditional upon union. Jesus is not teaching a formula for answered prayer; He is unveiling the mystery of desire transformed through abiding.

The Word as the Seed of Union

The Word of God is not merely instruction—it is life-bearing seed.

"The words that I speak to you are spirit, and they are life." (NKJV)

When the Word abides in a believer, it does not remain external. It penetrates, shapes, and realigns the inner life. The Word carries the very nature, will, and mind of God. To abide in the Word is to allow God's thought-life to dwell within you.

This is why intimacy with the Lord cannot be sustained without Scripture—not as information to be studied alone, but as life to be received.

Abiding in the Word vs. Knowing the Word

There is a crucial difference between knowing Scripture and abiding in it.

- Knowledge informs the mind
- Abiding transforms the heart

The Pharisees knew the Scriptures yet remained disconnected from the Life they testified of.

"You search the Scriptures, for in them you think you have eternal life; and these are they which testify of Me." (NKJV)

The Word was meant to lead into union with Christ, not replace it.

How the Word Abides in the Believer

The Word abides when it is:

- Received with humility
- Meditated on with openness

- Obeyed with surrender
- Trusted beyond understanding

"Your word I have hidden in my heart, that I might not sin against You." (NKJV)

To hide the Word in the heart is to make it the governing voice within. Where the Word abides, sin loses dominance—not through effort, but through displacement.

Desire Transformed Through Union

Jesus makes a stunning connection between abiding and desire:

"You will ask what you desire..." (NKJV)

This does not mean every natural desire is automatically fulfilled. It means desire itself is reshaped.

When the Word abides:

- Self-centered desires are purified
- Fleshly cravings lose authority
- God's desires are birthed within

Prayer becomes the expression of shared longing, not personal ambition.

This is the mystery:

When union is real, God's will becomes the believer's desire.

Prayer as the Language of Union

Prayer is not an attempt to persuade God—it is the conversation of those already united.

"The effective, fervent prayer of a righteous man avails much." (NKJV)

Righteousness here is not moral perfection—it is right standing and right alignment. Prayer that flows from union carries authority because it originates from intimacy.

When the Word abides, prayer changes:

- From asking to agreeing
- From striving to resting
- From repetition to resonance

Prayer becomes intercourse of the will, where divine intention flows through human voice.

Why Many Prayers Go Unanswered

Unanswered prayer is often not a lack of faith—it is a lack of abiding.

"You ask and do not receive, because you ask amiss, that you may spend it on your pleasures." (NKJV)

Where the Word does not abide, desire remains misaligned. God's silence is not rejection—it is protection. He refuses to empower what would weaken union.

Answered prayer flows naturally where desire and Word are one.

The Word as the Boundary of Intimacy

Love without truth becomes sentimentality. Truth without love becomes legalism. The Word preserves intimacy by setting holy boundaries.

"Sanctify them by Your truth. Your word is truth." (NKJV)

Sanctification is not separation from God—it is separation unto God. The Word removes what contaminates communion so that intimacy remains pure, safe, and life-giving.

Abiding in the Word and Freedom

True freedom is not independence—it is alignment.

"And you shall know the truth, and the truth shall make you free." (NKJV)

Freedom comes when the Word liberates the believer from self-deception, fear, and control. The Word frees not by information, but by indwelling presence.

Where the Word abides, the believer lives from rest, not pressure.

The Word and Continual Intercourse

Spiritual intercourse with the Lord is sustained by:

- Listening
- Receiving
- Responding

The Word initiates, the Spirit applies, and the believer participates. This is not episodic—it is continuous communion.

"Man shall not live by bread alone, but by every word that proceeds from the mouth of God." (NKJV)

Life flows from ongoing reception, not past encounters.

The Fruit of a Word-Abiding Life

Where the Word abides:

- Discernment increases
- Prayer deepens

- Peace governs
- Obedience becomes joyful

The believer no longer chases answers—answers flow naturally from union.

Why This Chapter Is Crucial

Without the Word abiding:

- Abiding becomes emotional
- Prayer becomes selfish
- Desire becomes distorted

With the Word abiding:

- Intimacy is stabilized
- Desire is purified
- Prayer is empowered

The Word does not replace the Spirit.

The Spirit does not bypass the Word.

Together, they preserve union.

Where We Go Next

The Word aligns desire.

Now love must preserve obedience.

CHAPTER TWELVE: ABIDE IN MY LOVE — OBEDIENCE AS THE SAFEGUARD OF UNION

(John 15:10)

Union with God is sustained by love, but love is preserved through obedience. This is one of the most misunderstood truths in the Christian life. Obedience is often treated as legalism, restriction, or religious duty, yet Jesus presents it as the protective boundary of intimacy. Obedience does not create union—it keeps union unobstructed.

"If you keep My commandments, you will abide in My love, just as I have kept My Father's commandments and abide in His love." (NKJV)

This statement places obedience not in the realm of law, but in the realm of love and union. Jesus does not say obedience earns love; He says obedience maintains abiding.

Obedience Is Relational, Not Legal

Biblical obedience is not compliance to impersonal rules; it is response to a Person.

- Law-based obedience fears punishment
- Love-based obedience protects intimacy

Jesus grounds His call to obedience in His own relationship with the Father.

"I always do those things that please Him." (NKJV)

This is not performance—it is relational alignment. Jesus obeyed not to earn the Father's love, but because He lived in the Father's love.

Why Love Without Obedience Fails

Love that refuses obedience becomes sentimental and unstable. Scripture never separates love from obedience because disobedience always introduces distance.

"He who has My commandments and keeps them, it is he who loves Me." (NKJV)

Disobedience does not end union positionally, but it fractures fellowship experientially. The Spirit remains, but communion is clouded. The flow of life is hindered—not because God withdraws, but because the heart resists alignment.

Obedience as the Guardian of Intimacy

Obedience functions like a guardrail. It does not restrict movement; it preserves safety.

"Great peace have those who love Your law, and nothing causes them to stumble." (NKJV)

Peace is the byproduct of alignment. Anxiety, confusion, and unrest often signal misalignment, not divine absence. Obedience restores clarity because it restores flow.

The Pattern: Christ's Obedience as the Model of Union

Jesus presents His own obedience as the pattern believers are to follow.

"Just as I have kept My Father's commandments and abide in His love." (NKJV)

Here we see the deepest truth: obedience is how love abides.

Christ's obedience:

- Was voluntary
- Was joyful
- Was relational
- Was continuous

This obedience carried Him through suffering, rejection, and the cross—without severing union.

"Father, into Your hands I commit My spirit." (NKJV)

Even in death, communion remained unbroken.

The Difference Between Obedience and Works

Works seek to achieve righteousness.

Obedience flows from relationship.

"For this is the love of God, that we keep His commandments. And His commandments are not burdensome." (NKJV)

If obedience feels burdensome, love has been displaced by fear or self-effort. Where love governs, obedience becomes natural, not forced.

Obedience and the Crucified Will

True obedience requires the death of self-rule.

"Not My will, but Yours, be done." (NKJV)

This is the essence of abiding love. The will of God is not imposed; it is embraced. Union deepens where the will yields. Resistance does not make us free—it makes us fragmented.

Why Disobedience Disrupts Spiritual Intercourse

Spiritual intercourse with God requires openness, trust, and surrender. Disobedience introduces:

- Secrecy
- Justification
- Self-protection

These hinder intimacy.

"If I regard iniquity in my heart, the Lord will not hear." (NKJV)

This does not mean God becomes deaf; it means the channel is obstructed. Obedience clears the channel, so communion remains unhindered.

Obedience and Holiness

Holiness is not withdrawal from God—it is alignment with God.

"Be holy, for I am holy." (NKJV)

Holiness protects intimacy by removing what contaminates union. God does not call us to holiness to distance us from Himself, but to prepare us for deeper communion.

The Joy of Obedience

Jesus reveals the outcome of abiding obedience:

"These things I have spoken to you, that My joy may remain in you, and that your joy may be full." (NKJV)

Joy is not the reward of self-expression; it is the fruit of alignment. Obedience keeps joy intact because joy flows from unbroken union.

Obedience Within the Body

Obedience is not only personal—it is corporate.

"Submitting to one another in the fear of God." (NKJV)

Mutual submission preserves unity. Where obedience to love is rejected, division follows. Where obedience is embraced, the Body remains healthy and life circulates freely.

Why This Chapter Is Essential

Without obedience:

- Love becomes emotional
- Intimacy becomes inconsistent
- Union becomes theoretical

With obedience:

- Love remains active
- Intimacy is protected
- Union is sustained

Obedience is not the enemy of intimacy—

disobedience is.

The Flow Forward

The Word aligns desire.

Love sustains obedience.

Obedience preserves union.

Now we move into the visible expression of abiding love:

CHAPTER THIRTEEN: WALKING IN THE LIGHT — FELLOWSHIP, CLEANSING, AND UNION

(1 John 1:7)

Union with God does not thrive in concealment. It flourishes in light. Light is the environment in which intimacy is sustained, fellowship is preserved, and communion remains unbroken. The apostle John does not describe light merely as moral correctness, but as relational transparency before God. To walk in the light is to live openly, honestly, and continually before the Lord.

"But if we walk in the light as He is in the light, we have fellowship with one another, and the blood of Jesus Christ His Son cleanses us from all sin." (NKJV)

This single verse unveils a profound mystery: light, fellowship, and cleansing are inseparable realities. Where one is present, the others follow.

Light Is God's Dwelling Environment

Scripture consistently reveals that God does not merely give light—He is light.

"God is light and in Him is no darkness at all." (NKJV)

Light is not something God uses; it is the nature of His presence. To walk with God is therefore to walk in light. Darkness is not merely sin—it is distance from transparency. Where darkness is tolerated, intimacy is compromised.

Walking in the Light Is Relational, Not Performative

John does not say, "If we are perfect," but "If we walk." Walking implies process, movement, and direction.

Walking in the light means:

- Living honestly before God
- Refusing hidden compartments
- Allowing the Spirit to expose without resistance
- Responding to conviction without defense

This is not sinless perfection—it is unhidden relationship.

"He who walks uprightly walks securely." (NKJV)

Security flows from transparency. Fear thrives in concealment; peace thrives in light.

Fellowship: The Shared Life of Union

John declares that walking in the light produces fellowship.

"We have fellowship with one another..." (NKJV)

Fellowship here is not social interaction—it is shared life. The Greek word carries the idea of participation, communion, and mutual possession. Fellowship is the horizontal expression of vertical union.

Union with God that does not produce fellowship with others is incomplete. Light restores both:

- Fellowship with God
- Fellowship with the Body

Darkness fractures both simultaneously.

Why Light Is Necessary for Union

Union requires trust, and trust requires openness. Darkness introduces:

- Shame
- Fear
- Self-protection
- Justification

These are barriers to intimacy.

"Everyone practicing evil hates the light and does not come to the light, lest his deeds should be exposed." (NKJV)

Light does not condemn—it reveals. What light reveals, the blood cleanses. What darkness conceals, remains untreated.

The Blood of Jesus — Continual Cleansing in Light

John does not say the blood has cleansed only, but that it cleanses.

"The blood of Jesus Christ His Son cleanses us from all sin." (NKJV)

This is present, ongoing action. The blood is not only for conversion—

it is for continual fellowship. As believers walk in the light, the blood keeps the channel of union clear.

This does not minimize holiness—it empowers it.

Light and Confession

Walking in the light naturally leads to confession—not as ritual, but as relational honesty.

"If we confess our sins, He is faithful and just to forgive us our sins and to cleanse us from all unrighteousness." (NKJV)

Confession is not informing God—He already knows. Confession is agreeing with God. Agreement restores alignment. Alignment restores flow. Flow preserves intimacy.

Darkness as the Interruption of Spiritual Intercourse

Spiritual intercourse with God requires openness and trust. Darkness interrupts this exchange.

Darkness may include:

- Unconfessed sin
- Hidden resentment
- Justified disobedience
- Secret independence

These do not remove the Spirit, but they grieve Him.

"Do not grieve the Holy Spirit of God." (NKJV)

Grief does not mean abandonment—it means wounded fellowship.

Light Preserves the Tenderness of the Heart

Walking in the light keeps the heart soft and responsive.

"Today, if you will hear His voice, do not harden your hearts." (NKJV)

Hardness develops when conviction is resisted. Softness is preserved when light is welcomed. A soft heart remains sensitive to the Spirit, quick to repent, and open to correction.

Light and Freedom

Light does not enslave—it liberates.

"You shall know the truth, and the truth shall make you free." (NKJV)

Freedom is not the ability to hide—it is the courage to be fully known. Where light reigns, shame loses its power. Where shame is removed, intimacy deepens.

Walking in the Light as a Way of Life

Walking in the light is not an event—it is a lifestyle of openness.

This includes:

- Honest prayer
- Transparent relationships
- Immediate repentance
- Continual dependence

"Search me, O God, and know my heart; try me, and know my anxieties." (NKJV)

This is not fear—it is trust.

The Fruit of Walking in the Light

Where believers walk in the light:

- Fellowship remains strong
- Cleansing remains continual
- Intimacy remains unhindered
- Union remains experiential

Light does not expose to shame—it exposes to heal.

Why This Chapter Is Crucial

Without light:

- Union becomes positional only
- Fellowship becomes superficial
- Obedience becomes selective

With light:

- Union becomes lived
- Fellowship becomes deep
- Cleansing becomes continual

Walking in the light is not about perfection—it is about presence without hiding.

The Journey Continues

Abiding teaches communion.

The Word aligns desire.

Love preserves obedience.

Light sustains fellowship.

Now we move into the evidence of indwelling union:

CHAPTER FOURTEEN: GOD ABIDES IN US — LOVE PERFECTED, ASSURANCE ESTABLISHED, UNION SEALED

(1 John 4:12–13)

At this point in our journey, Scripture presses us beyond experience into assurance, beyond intimacy into permanence. The apostle John now addresses a crucial question that every believer faces—How do we know that union with God is real, present, and enduring? The answer is not found in emotion, memory, or outward activity, but in God abiding in us by His Spirit, with love perfected as the evidence.

"No one has seen God at any time. If we love one another, God abides in us, and His love has been perfected in us." (NKJV)

"By this we know that we abide in Him, and He in us, because He has given us of His Spirit." (NKJV)

These verses take us to the deepest layer of intimacy—where union is no longer questioned but known.

From Encounter to Indwelling Assurance

Many believers know God through encounters, moments, or seasons. But John speaks of something deeper: abiding certainty. He uses the language of knowing, not guessing.

"By this we know..." (NKJV)

This knowledge is not intellectual; it is relational assurance. It is the settled awareness that God is not merely near, but within—not occasionally present but permanently abiding.

Assurance flows from union, not from performance.

Why John Connects Indwelling to Love

John does not say, "If we have knowledge," or "If we have power," but:

"If we love one another..." (NKJV)

Love is the clearest manifestation of God's indwelling life because love cannot be sustained by human effort alone. Natural affection fades. Divine love endures. When love persists—especially in difficulty—it reveals a source beyond the self.

Love is not merely commanded; it is imparted.

Perfected Love — Not Flawless Love, but Complete Love

When John speaks of love being perfected, he does not mean sinless emotion or uninterrupted feeling.

"His love has been perfected in us." (NKJV)

Perfected love means:

- Love that has reached its intended goal
- Love that flows freely without fear
- Love that completes the circuit from God → believer → others

Perfected love is love that no longer stops with the self.

God Unseen, Yet Made Visible

John makes a remarkable statement:

"No one has seen God at any time." (NKJV)

Yet immediately follows with the implication that God becomes visible through love.

When believers love:

- God is revealed
- God is manifested
- God is made known

The invisible God chooses to express Himself through an indwelt people. Love is the incarnation continued through the Church.

The Spirit as the Seal of Union

John anchors assurance not in human behavior, but in divine action.

"Because He has given us of His Spirit." (NKJV)

The Spirit is not merely comforter or helper—He is the seal of union. A seal signifies ownership, permanence, and authenticity. God does not lend His Spirit temporarily; He gives Him as a pledge.

Where the Spirit abides:

- Union is established
- Assurance is internal
- Communion is living

The Witness Within

Scripture speaks of an internal testimony.

"The Spirit Himself bears witness with our spirit that we are children of God." (NKJV)

This witness is not emotional hype—it is quiet certainty. It does not shout; it settles. It does not argue; it assures. This is why believers can endure trials without losing intimacy—because assurance is rooted internally, not circumstantially.

Why Fear Cannot Coexist with Perfected Love

Later in the same passage, John declares:

"There is no fear in love; but perfect love casts out fear." (NKJV)

Fear thrives where union is questioned. Fear diminishes where assurance is established. Perfected love does not eliminate reverence—it eliminates dread, insecurity, and performance-driven religion.

Fear asks, "Am I accepted?"

Love declares, "I am indwelt."

Indwelling Love and Obedience

Where God abides, obedience flows naturally.

"If we love Him, we keep His commandments." (NKJV)

This is not compulsion—it is alignment. The Spirit does not force obedience; He forms desire. Obedience becomes the expression of shared life, not an attempt to earn approval.

Union That Produces Confidence, Not Presumption

Assurance does not lead to carelessness—it leads to confidence rooted in humility.

"Herein is our love made perfect, that we may have boldness in the day of judgment." (NKJV)

Boldness here is not arrogance; it is confidence born of union. The believer stands secure not because of flawless conduct, but because of indwelling life.

Why This Chapter Is a Turning Point

This chapter marks a shift:

- From striving to resting
- From doubt to assurance
- From effort to evidence

Union is no longer something to prove—it is something to live from.

Without this revelation:

- Believers remain uncertain
- Intimacy becomes fragile
- Love becomes conditional

With this revelation:

- Assurance becomes stable

- Intimacy becomes deep
- Love becomes fearless

The Flow Continues

Abiding teaches communion.

Love perfects assurance.

The Spirit seals union.

Now John takes us even further—into the confession of Christ, the source of victory, and the overcoming life.

CHAPTER FIFTEEN: CONFESSING THE SON — UNION, VICTORY, AND OVERCOMING THE WORLD

(1 John 4:15–21; 1 John 5:3–4)

Union with God does not remain hidden. What is indwelt inwardly must be confessed outwardly. The apostle John now brings intimacy to its public and victorious expression: confession of the Son. Confession is not mere verbal agreement with doctrine; it is the outflow of union, the testimony of an indwelling reality that cannot remain silent.

Where Christ truly abides, confession becomes inevitable, and where confession is living, victory over the world follows.

Confession as the Evidence of Indwelling

John writes with clarity and assurance:

"Whoever confesses that Jesus is the Son of God, God abides in him, and he in God." (NKJV)

Confession here is not ritual recitation. It is revelatory agreement. To confess Jesus as the Son of God is to align the heart, mind, and life with God's eternal testimony concerning His Son.

This confession reveals:

- Submission to divine truth
- Participation in divine life
- Identification with divine authority

Where this confession is real, union is active.

Why Confession Is Necessary for Union to Remain Active

Union is relational, not mechanical. Love desires expression, and truth demands witness.

"And we have known and believed the love that God has for us." (NKJV)

Notice the order: known and believed. Knowledge alone is insufficient. Belief alone is incomplete. Confession unites both and releases them into life.

What is not confessed will eventually be suppressed. What is confessed is strengthened and established.

Confession Anchored in Love, Not Fear

John immediately grounds confession in love:

"God is love, and he who abides in love abides in God, and God in him." (NKJV)

Confession driven by fear seeks safety.

Confession driven by love seeks faithfulness.

Love does not confess Christ to avoid judgment—it confesses Christ because union has already been established.

Perfected Love Produces Boldness

John connects love, union, and confidence:

"Love has been perfected among us in this: that we may have boldness in the day of judgment; because as He is, so are we in this world." (NKJV)

This is one of the most staggering declarations in Scripture.

Union produces likeness.

Likeness produces confidence.

Confidence produces boldness.

Boldness is not presumption—it is shared identity. The believer stands without fear because union has replaced separation.

Fear as a Sign of Broken Assurance

John is uncompromising:

"There is no fear in love; but perfect love casts out fear, because fear involves torment." (NKJV)

Fear thrives where union is doubted. Torment exists where assurance is fragile. Perfected love removes fear not by ignoring holiness, but by establishing belonging.

Fear asks, "Am I accepted?"

Love declares, "I am indwelt."

Love Expressed Toward God and Others

John brings confession into practical reality:

"If someone says, 'I love God,' and hates his brother, he is a liar." (NKJV)

Union with God cannot coexist with hatred toward others because love flows from one source. Love is the circulation of divine life. To block it in one direction is to disrupt it everywhere.

"And this commandment we have from Him: that he who loves God must love his brother also." (NKJV)

Love is not optional—it is the law of union.

Overcoming the World — The Fruit of Union

John now shifts from assurance to victory:

"For this is the love of God, that we keep His commandments. And His commandments are not burdensome." (NKJV)

Obedience becomes light where love governs. But John goes further:

"For whatever is born of God overcomes the world." (NKJV)

Victory is not achieved—it is inherited. Overcoming is not the result of effort; it is the result of new birth and union.

Faith as the Mechanism of Victory

John clarifies the means:

"And this is the victory that has overcome the world—our faith." (NKJV)

Faith here is not optimism or mental agreement. Faith is relational trust rooted in union. Faith overcomes the world because it draws from a life greater than the world.

The world system thrives on:

- Lust of the flesh
- Lust of the eyes
- Pride of life

Union with Christ renders these powerless.

Why the World Cannot Overcome the United Believer

The world can pressure, tempt, threaten, and deceive—but it cannot overcome divine life.

"Who is he who overcomes the world, but he who believes that Jesus is the Son of God?" (NKJV)

Belief here is not abstract—it is relational allegiance. To believe in the Son is to live from His life. The world cannot conquer what it cannot supply.

Confession as Warfare

Confession is not passive—it is spiritual warfare. To confess Christ in a hostile world is to declare allegiance to a different kingdom.

"If you confess with your mouth the Lord Jesus and believe in your heart that God has raised Him from the dead, you will be saved." (NKJV)

Confession reinforces salvation not by earning it, but by aligning life with truth.

Union That Produces a Conquering Life

Union does not produce escape from the world—it produces victory within it.

- Temptation loses authority
- Fear loses dominance
- Sin loses attraction
- The world loses its grip

Not because the believer is strong, but because Christ lives within.

Why This Chapter Is Critical

Without confession:

- Union becomes private and fragile
- Love becomes theoretical
- Victory becomes elusive

With confession:

- Union becomes public and strong
- Love becomes visible
- Victory becomes normal

Confession does not create union.

Union demands confession.

The Journey Nears Completion

Union produces abiding.

Abiding produces love.

Love produces assurance.

Assurance produces confession.

Confession releases victory.

Now we come to one of the deepest personal declarations of union in all of Scripture:

FINAL THEOLOGICAL CONCLUSION

Becoming One Forever — The Consummation of Union

All theology, when rightly understood, does not terminate in explanation—it culminates in union. The Scriptures do not merely inform the mind; they draw the soul back into God's eternal intention. From the first breath in Genesis to the final declaration in Revelation, the Word of God reveals one unbroken divine purpose: God desires to dwell with humanity in oneness.

This book has traced that purpose carefully, reverently, and progressively. What now remains is to gather every thread into a single, radiant truth.

Union Was Not God's Response — It Was God's Intention

Union with God was not conceived after the fall. It was not a redemptive improvisation. It was the original design.

- Creation revealed union
- The fall fractured communion
- Covenant preserved the promise
- The incarnation restored union
- The Spirit made union personal
- The Church expressed union corporately
- The cross sealed union permanently

Redemption does not elevate humanity beyond its design—it returns humanity to it.

"According as He hath chosen us in Him before the foundation of the world..." (NKJV)

This is not theological ornamentation. It is divine architecture.

Why Union Required the Language of Marriage and the Reality of Intercourse

God chose no higher earthly analogy than marriage to reveal union because marriage alone speaks of:

- Covenant, not contract
- Exchange of life, not proximity
- Permanence, not visitation
- Fruitfulness, not productivity

The Scriptures do not shy away from this language because God is not embarrassed by His own design. Physical union was created to teach spiritual reality. Sexual intercourse, within covenant, reveals the mystery of oneness through self-giving love.

"This is a great mystery, but I speak concerning Christ and the church." (NKJV)

To strip marriage of its theological meaning is to obscure God's revelation. To strip intimacy with God of its depth is to settle for religion instead of union.

Intercourse as the Highest Expression of Union

Throughout this work, the word intercourse has been used deliberately—not to provoke carnality, but to restore biblical weight.

Intercourse means:

- Exchange of life
- Mutual yielding
- Shared essence
- Ongoing participation

Spiritual intercourse is not mystical excess—it is biblical normality.

"He who is joined to the Lord is one spirit with Him." (NKJV)

This is not metaphor. This is ontology.

Christianity is not belief about God.

It is participation in God.

Why Independence Is the Last Enemy of Intimacy

At the heart of the fall was independence—the desire to live from self rather than from God. At the heart of redemption is the death of that independence.

"I have been crucified with Christ; it is no longer I who live, but Christ lives in me." (NKJV)

This is not loss of identity—it is fulfillment of identity. Humanity was never designed to be autonomous. Autonomy produces anxiety. Union produces rest.

The most mature Christian life is not the most self-sufficient one—it is the most God-dependent one.

The Church as the Corporate Fulfillment of Union

Union is not only personal; it is corporate and eschatological.

The Church is not a gathering of individuals—it is:

- One Body
- One Spirit
- One Life
- One Bride

"That they all may be one, as You, Father, are in Me, and I in You." (NKJV)

Disunity in the Church is not merely organizational failure—it is theological contradiction. The Church exists to manifest on earth what is true in heaven: oneness in Christ.

The Spirit as the Guarantee of Eternal Consummation

The indwelling Spirit is not only the source of present intimacy—He is the pledge of future union.

"Who also has sealed us and given us the Spirit in our hearts as a guarantee." (NKJV)

What is now known by faith will one day be known by sight. What is now experienced inwardly will one day be revealed outwardly. The Bride who knows the Bridegroom now by the Spirit will meet Him face to face.

From Abiding to Appearing

Scripture ends where it began—with God dwelling with humanity.

"Behold, the tabernacle of God is with men, and He will dwell with them." (NKJV)

Eternity is not escape from creation—it is creation fully indwelt by God. Heaven and earth are not separated forever; they are reunited in Christ. The final state is not disembodied spirituality, but glorified union.

Union does not dissolve humanity.

It glorifies it.

The Final Truth

Intimacy with the Lord is not a spiritual luxury.

It is not reserved for mystics, leaders, or the mature few.

It is the inheritance of every believer.

God does not desire servants who merely obey Him.

He desires sons who abide in Him.

He does not seek a distant people.

He seeks a dwelling place.

The Great Mystery, Fully Revealed

What began as spirit and soul in eternity…

What was taught through flesh and marriage…

What was restored through Christ and the cross…

What is lived now by the Spirit…

Will be consummated forever in glory.

One God

One Christ

One Spirit

One Body

One Bride

One Life

This is the mystery.

This is the gospel.

This is INTIMACY WITH THE LORD.

FINAL PRAYER

A Prayer of Union, Surrender, and Eternal Oneness

Holy and Eternal Father,

Source of life, Fountain of love, Dwelling place of all truth—

We come not as strangers, but as those You have called, chosen, and drawn into Yourself

before the foundation of the world.

We stand in awe of Your eternal purpose:

not merely to save us from sin,

but to bring us back into union with You.

Thank You for Jesus Christ,

the Word made flesh,

who entered our humanity to restore what was lost,

who bore our separation so we might share Your life,

who loved us and gave Himself for us (NKJV).

Thank You for the cross,

where the old self was crucified,

where independence died,

and where a new life began—

"It is no longer I who live, but Christ lives in me" (NKJV).

Holy Spirit,

we acknowledge You as the seal of our union,

the witness within our spirit,

the breath of divine life abiding in us.

Teach us to yield fully,

to grieve You no longer,

to walk in the light as You are in the light (NKJV).

Father, we surrender every place of resistance—

every hidden fear,

every desire for control,

every form of self-rule

that interrupts communion with You.

We choose the cross.

We choose dependence.

We choose abiding.

Teach us to live not from effort, but from union.

Not from striving, but from shared life.

Not from duty, but from love perfected in us (NKJV).

Make our hearts a dwelling place where You are welcome without restriction.

Make our minds one with the mind of Christ.

Make our bodies temples yielded wholly to Your Spirit.

Make us one Body, one Bride, one people—

joined to the Lord as one Spirit (NKJV).

Let love flow freely—

love that casts out fear,

love that overcomes the world,

love that reveals the unseen God through visible lives (NKJV).

Prepare us as a Bride who knows her Bridegroom,

not only by doctrine,

but by intimacy.

Not only by confession,

but by communion.

And when Christ who is our life appears,

may we appear with Him in glory (NKJV),

having already learned to live from His life here and now.

We offer ourselves—

spirit, soul, and body—

as a living sacrifice, holy and acceptable to You (NKJV).

Receive us, Father.

Abide in us.

Live through us.

Until faith becomes sight,

until union is consummated in glory,

keep us abiding, loving, and one.

We ask this

not in our own name,

but in the name of Jesus Christ,

our Life, our Union, our Eternal Love.

AMEN

CLOSING EXHORTATION TO THE READER

Live the Union You Have Received

Beloved reader,

You have not merely read a book—you have been invited into a life. The truths unfolded in these pages are not meant to remain concepts admired from a distance. They are meant to be inhabited, lived, and embodied. Theology here does not end in understanding; it presses forward into union.

The call before you now is simple, yet weighty:

Live from what has already been given.

You were not saved to live near God.

You were saved to abide in Him.

You were not redeemed to strive toward intimacy.

You were redeemed to receive and remain in it.

"He who is joined to the Lord is one spirit with Him." (NKJV)

This is not a future hope alone—it is a present reality. The Christian life is not a climb toward God, but a walk with God from within. Every day, every moment, every breath is now an opportunity to choose dependence over independence, surrender over self-rule, communion over control.

Do not measure your life by activity.

Measure it by abiding.

When prayer feels dry, return to union.

When obedience feels heavy, return to love.

When fear whispers, return to assurance.

When the world presses, return to Christ who lives in you (NKJV).

Union does not remove trials—it reframes them.

Union does not silence suffering—it sustains you through it.

Union does not make you less human—it redeems your humanity.

Let your daily life become your sanctuary.

Let your ordinary moments become holy ground.

Let your choices flow not from pressure, but from presence.

Walk in the light.

Keep nothing hidden.

Yield quickly.

Love deeply.

Abide continually.

And remember this: maturity is not marked by how much you know, but by how fully Christ lives through you. The goal is not to appear spiritual, but to be indwelt. Not to perform righteousness, but to participate in divine life.

"As He is, so are we in this world." (NKJV)

This is your inheritance.

This is your calling.

This is your rest.

May you go forward not striving to become something new but resting in what you already are in Christ. May your life proclaim—without effort and without fear—that God has found His dwelling place.

Live the union.

Guard the intimacy.

Await the glory.

And until the day faith becomes sight,

abide in Him—always.

SCRIPTURE INDEX (NKJV)

INTIMACY WITH THE LORD

Genesis

- Genesis 1:26–27 — Humanity created in the image and likeness of God
- Genesis 2:7 — God breathes life into man
- Genesis 2:18–24 — One made two to become one flesh
- Genesis 3:6–10 — The fall and the loss of communion

Psalms

- Psalm 25:14 — The secret of the LORD with those who fear Him
- Psalm 51:6 — Truth in the inward parts

- Psalm 94:17 — The LORD as helper
- Psalm 119:105 — God's Word as light
- Psalm 119:165 — Peace for those who love God's law

Proverbs

- Proverbs 20:27 — The spirit of man as the lamp of the LORD

Ecclesiastes

- Ecclesiastes 3:11 — Eternity set in the human heart

Isaiah

- Isaiah 53:5–6 — The suffering Servant bearing sin
- Isaiah 57:15 — God dwelling with the contrite
- Isaiah 66:2 — God's dwelling with the humble

Jeremiah

- Jeremiah 31:33 — God's law written on the heart

Ezekiel

- Ezekiel 36:26–27 — A new heart and God's Spirit within
- Ezekiel 37:27 — God dwelling among His people

Matthew

- Matthew 5:48 — Call to divine completeness

- Matthew 19:4–6 — Jesus affirms Genesis and oneness
- Matthew 26:39 — "Not My will, but Yours be done"

John

- John 1:14 — The Word became flesh
- John 3:16 — God's love revealed in Christ
- John 6:63 — Words that are Spirit and life
- John 8:31–32 — Truth bringing freedom
- John 14:16–23 — The indwelling Spirit and mutual abiding
- John 15:1–10 — The vine, the branches, and abiding
- John 15:5–7 — Fruitfulness and prayer through union
- John 15:10 — Abiding in love through obedience
- John 17:5 — Christ's preexistent glory
- John 17:21–24 — The prayer for oneness

Acts

- Acts 2:1–4 — The outpouring of the Holy Spirit

Romans

- Romans 5:8 — God's love demonstrated in Christ
- Romans 8:1–17 — Life in the Spirit and sonship
- Romans 8:29–30 — Conformity to Christ

- Romans 12:1–2 — Living sacrifice and renewed mind

1 Corinthians

- 1 Corinthians 2:16 — The mind of Christ
- 1 Corinthians 3:16 — God's Spirit dwelling in believers
- 1 Corinthians 6:17 — One spirit with the Lord
- 1 Corinthians 10:16–17 — Participation in Christ
- 1 Corinthians 12:12–13 — One Body, one Spirit
- 1 Corinthians 13:1–13 — Love as the supreme virtue

2 Corinthians

- 2 Corinthians 3:16–18 — Transformation from glory to glory
- 2 Corinthians 5:17–21 — New creation and reconciliation

Galatians

- Galatians 2:20 — Crucified with Christ, Christ living in us
- Galatians 5:16–25 — Walking in the Spirit

Ephesians

- Ephesians 1:3–5 — Chosen in Christ before the foundation of the world
- Ephesians 2:13–22 — God dwelling with His people
- Ephesians 3:16–19 — Christ dwelling in the heart

- Ephesians 4:3–6 — One Spirit, one Body
- Ephesians 5:30–32 — Christ and the Church as one flesh

Philippians

- Philippians 2:5–11 — The mind and humility of Christ
- Philippians 4:6–7 — Peace guarding heart and mind

Colossians

- Colossians 1:27 — Christ in you, the hope of glory
- Colossians 3:3–4 — Christ as our life

Hebrews

- Hebrews 4:16 — Bold access to God
- Hebrews 10:19–22 — Entering the Holiest by the blood

James

- James 4:8 — Drawing near to God
- James 5:16 — Effective prayer

1 John

- 1 John 1:7–9 — Walking in the light and cleansing
- 1 John 2:3–6 — Knowing God through obedience
- 1 John 3:24 — God abiding in believers

- 1 John 4:7–21 — Love perfected through union
- 1 John 5:3–5 — Victory through faith

Revelation

- Revelation 19:7–9 — The marriage supper of the Lamb
- Revelation 21:2–3 — God dwelling with humanity
- Revelation 22:3–5 — Eternal communion with God

THEMATIC SCRIPTURE INDEX (NKJV)

INTIMACY WITH THE LORD

This thematic index groups the Scriptures used in this book according to core theological themes, allowing the reader to trace each doctrine from Genesis to Revelation and to use the book as a study, teaching, or meditation resource.

UNION WITH GOD / ONENESS

- Genesis 1:26–27
- Genesis 2:24
- Matthew 19:4–6
- John 17:21–24
- 1 Corinthians 6:17

- Ephesians 1:3–5
- Ephesians 5:30–32
- Colossians 1:27
- Galatians 2:20

INTIMACY & ABIDING

- Psalm 25:14
- John 14:16–23
- John 15:1–10
- John 15:5–7
- John 15:10
- 1 John 2:3–6
- 1 John 3:24

CREATION, DESIGN & PURPOSE

- Genesis 1:26–27
- Genesis 2:7
- Genesis 2:18–24
- Ecclesiastes 3:11
- Proverbs 20:27

THE FALL & SEPARATION

- Genesis 3:6–10
- Isaiah 59:2

- Romans 5:12
- Romans 8:6–8

REDEMPTION & RESTORATION

- Isaiah 53:5–6
- John 1:14
- 2 Corinthians 5:17–21
- Hebrews 10:19–22
- Colossians 3:3–4

THE INCARNATION

- John 1:14
- Philippians 2:5–11
- Hebrews 2:14
- 1 Timothy 3:16

THE INDWELLING HOLY SPIRIT

- John 14:16–17
- Acts 2:1–4
- Romans 8:9–16
- 1 Corinthians 3:16
- 1 Corinthians 6:19
- Ephesians 1:13–14

ONE BODY / THE CHURCH

- John 17:21
- 1 Corinthians 10:16–17
- 1 Corinthians 12:12–13
- Ephesians 2:13–22
- Ephesians 4:3–6
- Colossians 1:18

THE RENEWED MIND

- Romans 12:1–2
- 1 Corinthians 2:16
- Philippians 2:5
- Colossians 3:1–2

LOVE (DIVINE & PERFECTED)

- John 3:16
- Romans 5:8
- 1 Corinthians 13:1–13
- 1 John 4:7–21
- 1 John 5:1

OBEDIENCE & HOLINESS

- John 14:21
- John 15:10
- Romans 6:16–22

- 1 John 2:3–6
- 1 Peter 1:15–16

WALKING IN THE LIGHT

- Psalm 119:105
- John 8:12
- 1 John 1:7–9
- Ephesians 5:8–11

PRAYER & DESIRE ALIGNED WITH GOD

- Psalm 37:4
- John 15:7
- James 4:3
- James 5:16

CRUCIFIED LIFE / DEATH TO SELF

- Luke 9:23
- Romans 6:6–11
- Galatians 2:20
- Colossians 3:3

ASSURANCE & SONSHIP

- Romans 8:14–17
- 2 Corinthians 1:21–22
- 1 John 4:12–13

- 1 John 5:10–13

CONFESSION & WITNESS

- Romans 10:9–10
- 1 John 4:15
- Matthew 10:32

VICTORY & OVERCOMING THE WORLD

- John 16:33
- Romans 8:37
- 1 John 5:3–5

ETERNAL UNION / CONSUMMATION

- Revelation 19 :7–9
- Revelation 21:2–3
- Revelation 22:3–5

How to Use This Index

- For study: Trace one theme across Scripture
- For teaching: Build lessons around a single doctrine
- For devotion: Meditate on one theme per week
- For prayer: Turn each passage into personal communion with God

He who is joined to the Lord is one spirit with Him." (NKJV)

www.ingramcontent.com/pod-product-compliance
Lightning Source LLC
Chambersburg PA
CBHW022102050726
47591CB00002B/637

* 9 7 8 1 9 7 2 2 9 9 6 3 0 *